MY FIRST
WORDS

ENGLISH
ITALIAN

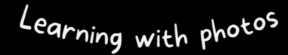

Learning with photos

The categories you will find in this book:

FAMILY → FAMIGLIA

Grandfather
Nonno

Grandmother
Nonna

Mother	Father	Aunt	Uncle
Madre	Padre	Zia	Zio

Sister	Brother	Cousin	Cousin
Sorella	Fratello	Cugino	Cugina

COLORS

Yellow

GIALLO

Blue

BLU

Orange

ARANCIONE

Purple

VIOLA

Brown

MARRONE

White

BIANCO

2

I COLORI

Beige

BEIGE

Black

NERO

Pink

ROSA

Red

ROSSO

Grey

GRIGIO

Green

VERDE

CLOTHES

T-shirt	Sweater	Pants

Maglietta	Maglione	Pantaloni

Shorts	Shoes	Hat

Pantaloncini	Scarpe	Cappello

Pyjamas	Swimsuit	Dress

Pigiama	Costume da bagno	Abito

I VESTITI

Cap

Cappellino

Beanie

Berretto

Gloves

Guanti

Scarf

Sciarpa

Glasses

Occhiali

Socks

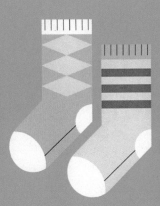

Calzini

Watch

Orologio da polso

Belt

Cintura

Hair clip

Fermaglio per capelli

ANIMALS

Cat	Dog	Bird

Gatto	Cane	Uccello

Mouse	Bee	Hamster

Topo	Ape	Criceto

Hen	Ladybug	Giraffe

Gallina	Coccinella	Giraffa

GLI ANIMALI

Tortoise	Pig	Snail

Tartaruga	Maiale	Lumaca

Sheep	Bear	Rabbit

Pecora	Orso	Coniglio

Whale	Dolphin	Butterfly

Balena	Delfino	Farfalla

Car	Subway	Truck

Auto	Metro	Camion

Bus	Taxi	Tractor

Autobus	Taxi	Trattore

Helicopter	Bike	Airplane
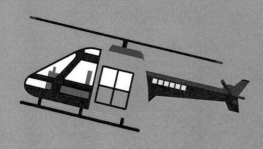		
Elicottero	Bici	Aereo

I TRANSPORTI

Boat

Barca

Rollerblades

Pattini a rotelle

Ambulance

Ambulanza

Train

Treno

Motorcycle

Moto

Scooter

Monopattino

Hot air balloon

Mongolfiera

Small boat

Barca

Submarine

Sottomarino

ZERO		One	
	ZERO		Uno

Two		Three	
	Due		Tre

Four		Five	
	Quattro		Cinqu

Six		Seven	
	Sei		Sette

Eight		Nine	
	Otto		Nove

English		Italiano
Monday		Lunedì
Tuesday		Martedì
Wednesday		Mercoledì
Thursday		Giovedì
Friday		Venerdì
Saturday		Sabato
Sunday	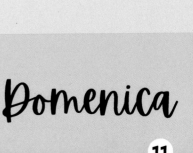	Domenica

FOOD

Fruits	Vegetables	Potatoes

Frutta	Verdure	Patate

Meat	Chicken	Egg

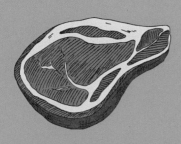  

Carne	Pollo	Uovo

Juice	Bread	Cereals

Succo	Pane	Cereali

GLI ALIMENTI

Yogurt

Yogurt

Milk

Latte

Cheese

Formaggio

Nuts

Noci

Legumes

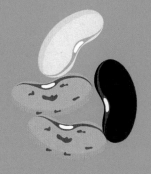

Leguminose

Tofu

Tofu

Dessert

Dessert

Soup

Zuppa

Pasta

Pasta

NATURE → NATURA

Tree	Flowers	Mountain

Albero	Fiori	Montagna

Leaf	Grass	Island
	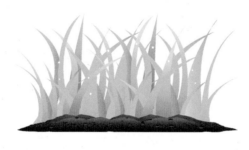	
Foglio	Erba	Isola

Plant	Soil	Desert

Pianta	Terra	Deserto

WEATHER → METEO

Sun	Cloud	Wind

Sole	Nuvola	Vente

Rainbow	Tornado	Ice

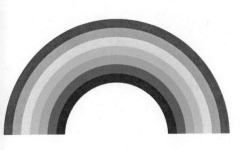  

Arcobaleno	Tornado	Ghiaccio

Rain	Snow	Thunderstorm

Pioggia	Neve	Temporale

15

Night

Notte

Star

Stella

Moon

Luna

Sky

Cielo

Planet

Pianeta

Earth

Terra

Comet

Cometa

Rocket

Razzo

Shooting star

Stella cadente

SEA → IL MARE

Sand

Sabbia

Parasol

Parasole

Starfish
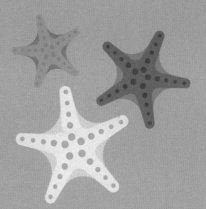
Stella marina

Beach towel

Asciugamano

Bucket

Secchio

Ball

Pallone

Water
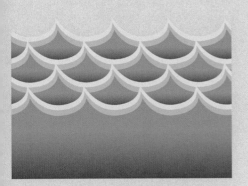
Acqua

Crab

Granchio

Fish

Pesce

17

MONTHS AND SEASONS

Gennaio
January

Febbraio
February

Marzo
March

Winter

Inverno

Ottobre
October

Novembre
November

Autunno

Autumn

Dicembre
December

I MESI E LE STAGIONI

Spring Primavera

Aprile
April

Maggio
May

Giugno
June

Summer Estate

Luglio
July

Agosto
August

Settembre
September

MUSIC → MUSICA

Piano

Violin

Guitar

Pianoforte

Violino

Chitarra

Saxophone

Triangle

Maracas

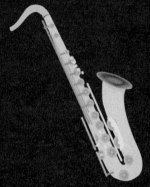

Sassofono

Triangolo

Maracas

Harp

Drum

Flute

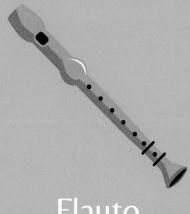

Arpa

Tamburo

Flauto

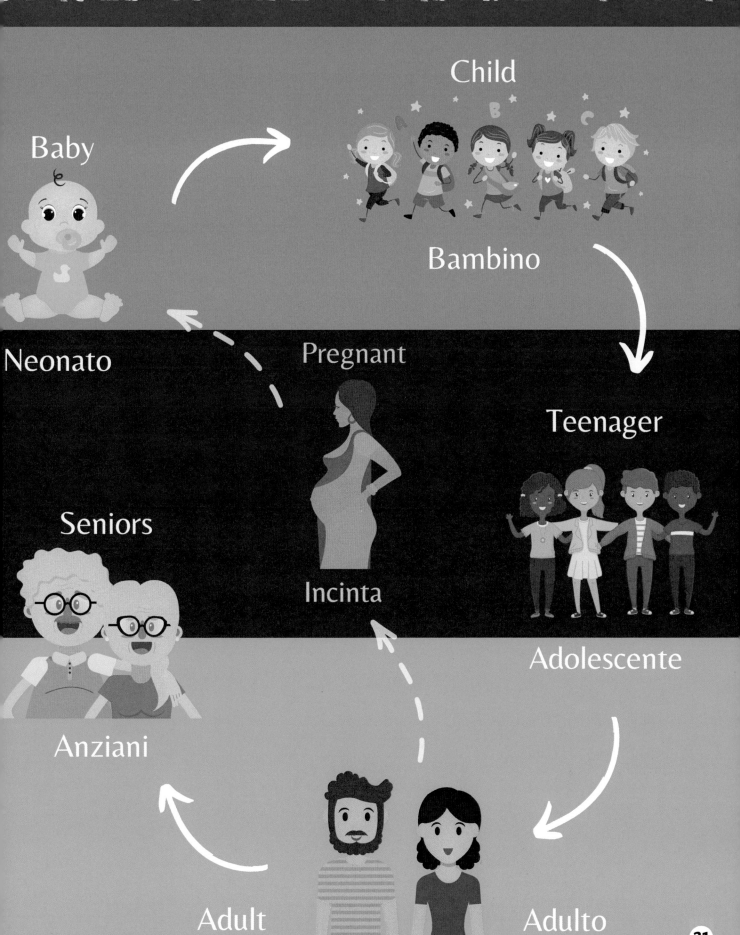

Child

Baby

Bambino

Neonato

Pregnant

Teenager

Seniors

Incinta

Anziani

Adolescente

Adult

AduIto

Adulto

21

SPORTS

Dance	Soccer	Tennis

Ballo	Calcio	Tennis

Gymnastics	Swimming	Golf

Ginnastica	Nuoto	Golf

Climbing	Judo	Basketball

Arrampicata	Judo	Basket

GLI SPORT

Ski	Surf	Kayak

Sci	Surf	Kayak

Ping-pong	Volleyball	Running

Ping-pong	Pallavolo	Corsa

Riding	Sailing	Skateboard

Equitazione	Vela	Skateboard

TRADES

Lawyer	Firefighter	Doctor

Avvocato	Pompiere	Dottore

Engineer	Nurse	Cook

Ingegnere	Infermiera	Cuoco

Scientist	Police officer	Dentist
		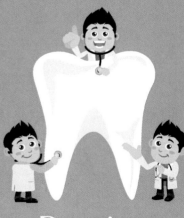
Scienziato	Agente di polizia	Dentista

LE PROFESSIONI

Painter

Pittore

Baker

Panettiere

Gardener

Giardiniere

Pilot

Pilota

Farmer

Agricoltore

Singer

Cantante

Detective

Detective

Veterinarian

Veterinario

Librarian

Bibliotecario

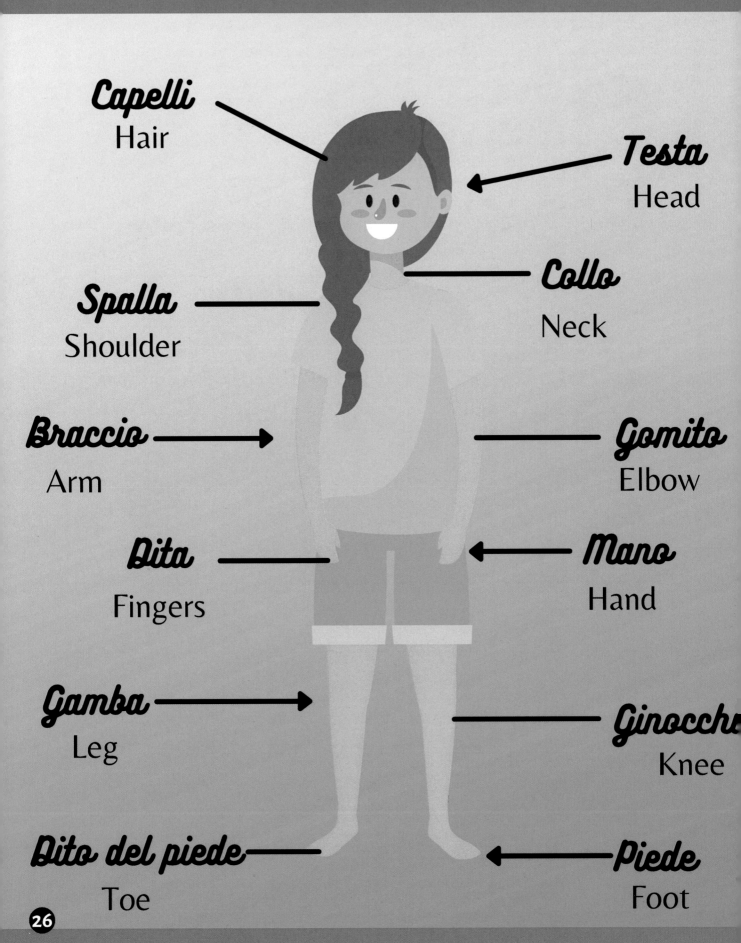

Capelli
Hair

Testa
Head

Spalla
Shoulder

Collo
Neck

Braccio
Arm

Gomito
Elbow

Dita
Fingers

Mano
Hand

Gamba
Leg

Ginocchio
Knee

Dito del piede
Toe

Piede
Foot

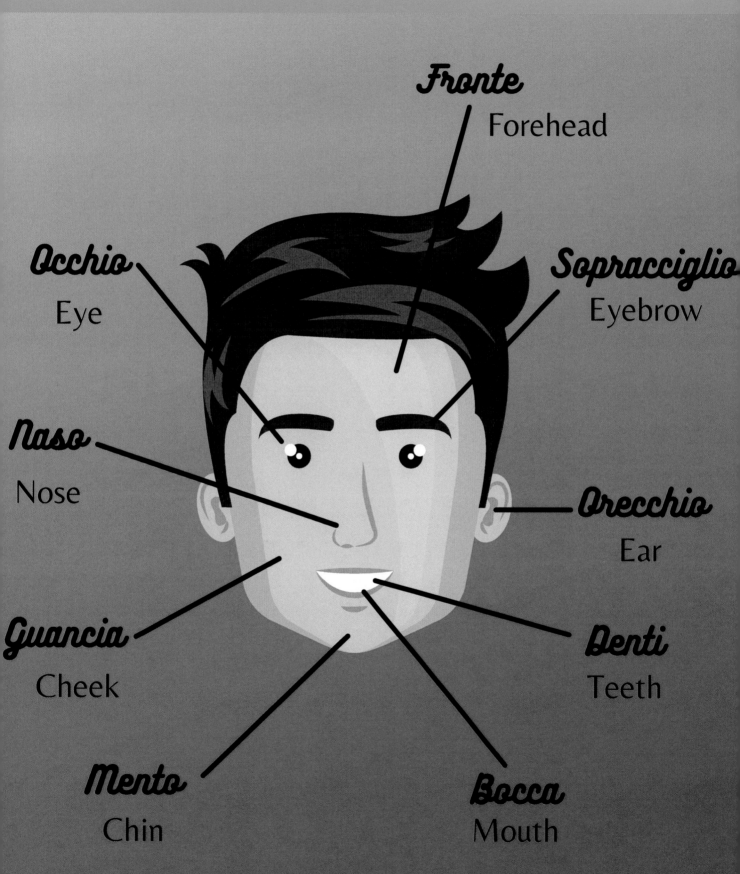

Fronte
Forehead

Occhio
Eye

Sopracciglio
Eyebrow

Naso
Nose

Orecchio
Ear

Guancia
Cheek

Denti
Teeth

Mento
Chin

Bocca
Mouth

SCHOOL SCUOLA

Teacher

Maestro/a

Corridor

Corridoio

Playground

Parco giochi

Notebook

Quaderno

Book

Libro

Paper

Carta

Board
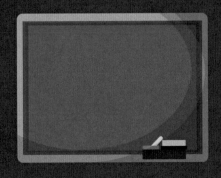
Lavagna

Backpack

Zaino

Desk
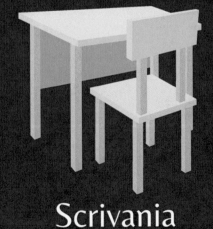
Scrivania

Scissors	Pencil sharpener	Chalk
Forbici	Tempera matite	Gesso

Glue	Ruler	Eraser
Colla	Righello	Gomma

Pen	Paintbrush	Pencil
Penna	Pennello	Matita

HOUSE

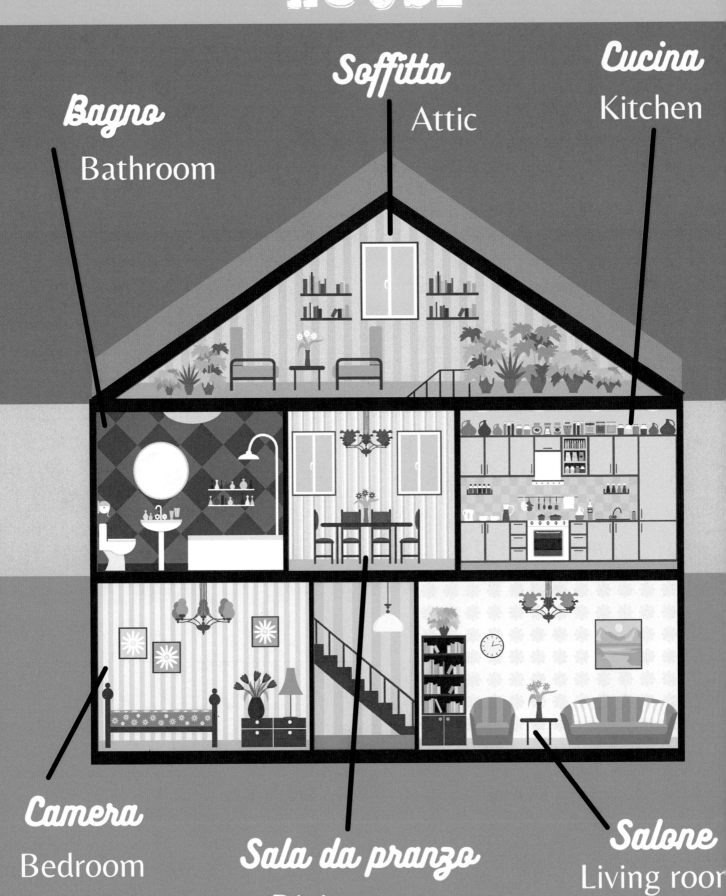

Bagno
Bathroom

Soffitta
Attic

Cucina
Kitchen

Camera
Bedroom

Sala da pranzo
Dining room

Salone
Living room

LA CASA

Toilet

Toilette

Shower

Doccia

Sofa

Divano

Chair

Sedia

Bed

Letto

Table

Tavolo

Television

Televisione

Wardrobe

Armadio

Bookcase

Biblioteca

ACTIONS

Eat	Sleep	Play

Mangiare	Dormire	Giocare

Study	Read	Wash

Studiare	Leggere	Lavare

Sing	Talk	Think

Cantare	Parlare	Pensare

LE AZIONI

Laugh

Ridere

Walk

Camminare

Get dressed

Vestirsi

Love

Amare

Dance

Ballare

Drive

Guidare

Run

Correre

Drink

Bere

Write

Scrivere

DIRECTIONS

Up  Alto

Left  Middle  Right

Centro

Sinistra

Destra

Down  Basso

LE DIREZIONI

North
Nord

East

West

Est

Ovest

South
Sud

DIETRO

AVANTI

IN FRONT OF

BEHIND

35

DAILY LIFE

Boy	Girl	Friends

Ragazzo	Ragazza	Amici

Vacation	Store	Nap

Vacanze	Negozio	Sonnellino

Hot	Cold	Sorry

Caldo	Freddo	Scusa

IL QUOTIDIANO

Yes	No	Well done !
Sì	No	Bravo !

Breakfast	Lunch	Dinner

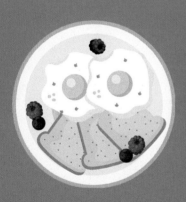  

Colazione	Pranzo	Cena

Hello	Goodbye	Thank you

Buongiorno	Arrivederci	Grazie

EMOTIONS → EMOZIONI

Tired	Sad	Angry

Stanco	Triste	Arrabbiato

Impressed	Happy	Anxious

Impressionato	Felice	Ansioso

In love	Sick	Surprised

Innamorato	Malato	Sorpreso

We hope you enjoyed the book and made some great discoveries!

Thanks !

Grazie !

PETITS CURIEUX EDITIONS

Made in the USA
Monee, IL
02 May 2022

95759706R00026